THE SPRINGER SPANIEL

WHO DIDN'T LIKE GETTING WET

Dave Martellaro

Dedication

I dedicate this book to my wife, Cherie, whose assistance, motivation, encouragement, and love guided me in getting these stories of Dasher down on paper for all children to enjoy.

About the Author

I was born in South Bend, Indiana, where I spent my childhood and much of my teenage years. I attended Northern Illinois University and have been in IT for what seems like all my life. I have always enjoyed telling stories, whether from books or making them up for children to engage their imaginations. My intention in writing these stories about Dasher's exploits was to capture and highlight important life lessons to help children deal with everyday life. Also, as a parent, I enjoyed sitting with my children and reading to them, as I hope this will also draw parents into reading to their children. When not working or writing, I enjoy watching college football and movies with Dashers' inspiration, my dog Loki.

Once upon a time, in a cozy neighborhood by a calm lake beside their house, lived a furry bundle of joy named Dasher with his father, Ben. Dasher was a Springer Spaniel puppy, full of life and mischief. Bouncy as a rubber band. A source of laughter and happiness for the family that they lived with. Including Mother, Father, Suzi, and Jimmy - all of whom adored him.

Dasher's dad, Ben, was no ordinary dog. He was a wise Springer Spaniel who had seen the world. He'd been around different places and had plenty of tales to tell. Ben had a twinkle in his eyes that said, "I know secrets."

Whenever he looked at Dasher, he saw a reflection of himself in his curious, fluffy pup.

Sunny days meant outdoor adventures. Days were brimming with laughter as Dasher dashed around the yard, chasing his tail, pouncing on leaves, leaping after butterflies, and discovering the wonders of the world. He especially loved his walks with Suzi under the warm sun, exploring every nook and cranny.

6

One day, as they were about to embark on their usual adventure, dark clouds gathered. The sky turned gray and heavy. Soon, raindrops began to fall, gently tapping the ground. Dasher stopped in his tracks, perplexed by the sudden change. Dasher's little nose twitched as he felt something cold and wet on his fur. Confused, he looked up at the sky, wondering what was happening.

As the raindrops started to patter down, Dasher's hesitation turned into a dash for cover. He scampered back to the porch, ears drooping and tail tucked, not too keen on the idea of getting wet. As he peeked out, he saw Ben standing outside under the rain, his fur wet and glistening like diamonds.

"Dasher, my son," Ben called out cheerily with a grin, "rain can be just as fun as sunshine! Come and see. Join the rain dance with Daddy."

"No, Dad, I don't like getting wet," Dasher whined.

Ben tried to get him back out in the rain with playful splashes. Ben showed Dasher how raindrops could turn into a merry dance on the ground and laughed like it was the best game in the world.

Dasher's curiosity got the better of him. He peered from the safety of the porch, intrigued by his father's antics. He cautiously stepped onto the wet ground, feeling the cool raindrops on his paws. "See, it's not so bad," Ben chuckled. It tickled a bit, like tiny little kisses from the sky.

Still unsure and with a puzzled look, Dasher joined Ben on the porch, watching as he shook off the rainwater with a twirl.

"See, Dad, the raindrops are too cold. I don't like it," Dasher howled.

Ben was an excellent water dog retriever and a champion swimmer. He zoomed through lakes, splashing and having a blast. He dreamt of teaching Dasher to swim, too, so they could splash and play together. But oh no! Dasher didn't like getting wet, not one bit. Ben was worried. How could he show Dasher that water could be fun?

Ben went into the bathroom and saw his owner drawing a bath for him. He had a brilliant idea! He hopped into the bathtub, filled with warm, bubbly water. Splish-splash! Ben enjoyed a bubble party all on his own.

"Dasher!" Ben called. "Come see how fun water can be!" Dasher peeked in, saw the bubbles, and laughed. He thought maybe water wasn't so scary.

After Ben was done, the owner added more bubbles. Dasher, curious, dipped a paw into the bubbly pool. It was warm and squishy! "Wow, this is cool!" Dasher said, smiling. He quickly hopped in. Bubbles tickled his fur, and he giggled. "Dad, you were right. Getting wet is fun!"

Ben grinned. "Dasher, you're a water pro now!" Dasher wiggled with joy. "But Dad, can we make water more fun?" he asked. "Of course!" Ben said.

At once, Ben thought of another idea. He loved to swim in the nearby lake, and he thought maybe the lake water could melt Dasher's fears away. The next day, they set off for the lake with a colorful floaty toy.

"Let's try the water," Ben suggested.

At the lakeshore, Dasher first eyed the water nervously. "Don't worry, my boy. This floater will keep you safe," Ben reassured. With a leap and a splash, Dasher found himself floating on the water, giggling as ripples formed around him. It felt like a soft bed on a gentle stream, and Dasher's worry floated away, too, with Ben's support.

From that day on, Dasher learned that water could be a friend. As the days went by, Dasher's love for water grew. Baths became a bubbly playground, and beach trips turned into epic adventures in the sand. With each new experience, Dasher learned that getting wet was endless fun. And guess what? Dasher even started enjoying rainy days with Suzi!

One sunny morning, while Dasher and Ben basked in the warmth, Dasher looked up at his father and said, "Dad, I used to be afraid of the rain. But rain isn't so scary. Thanks to you, I know that a little wetness can't stop the fun!"

And so, Dasher's adventures taught everyone an important lesson: We learn that trying new things might feel strange at first, but they can also be exciting. Just like Dasher, when we face our fears, we might find the coolest things waiting on the other side.